Trivial Pursuit™

OFFICIAL COMIC EDITION
BASED ON THE SILVER SCREEN® CARD SET

FEATURING HORN AND ABBOT

BY IAN AUSTIN & MARTIN KRANE

BANTAM BOOKS
TORONTO • NEW YORK • LONDON • SYDNEY • AUCKLAND

THE TRIVIAL PURSUIT OFFICIAL COMIC EDITION BASED ON THE SILVER SCREEN CARD SET

A Bantam Book/November 1984

Trivial Pursuit®

is a registered trademark of Horn Abbot Ltd., Box 1630, Niagara on the Lake, Ontario, Canada, LOS1JO

ISBN 0-553-34186-3

Published simultaneously in the United States and Canada

Bantam Books are published by Bantam Books, Inc. Its trademark consisting of the words "Bantam Books" and the portrayal of a rooster, is Registered in U.S. Patent and Trademark Office and in other countries. Marca Registrada. Bantam Books, Inc. 666 Fifth Avenue, New York, New York 10103.

PRINTED IN THE UNITED STATES OF AMERICA

KP 0 9 8 7 6 5 4 3 2 1

Q. WHO ARE HORN AND ABBOT?

A. SEE BELOW.

At last! The book you've been waiting for—***The Trivial Pursuit™ Comic Edition,*** the only authorized volume based on the Trivial Pursuit Silver Screen Edition featuring Horn and Abbot. And who are Horn and Abbot? Good question!

The Answer: Horn and Abbot, the two moustachioed characters who inhabit each comic adventure, represent, in fact, *three* men.

In 1979, a bright young photo editor named Chris Haney (a.k.a. "Horn") joined forces with sports writer Scott Abbott (a.k.a. "Abbot") to create the board game ***Trivial Pursuit™,*** one of the most popular games in history. They were soon joined by Chris' puck-plying brother John (a.k.a. "Clone Horn") and the curious three set out to ask and answer the questions appearing in those well-known silver boxes. And as long as there's a question unanswered, Horn and Abbot will ask it.

Aiding Horn and Abbot in their quest for trivial knowledge are the info-ravenous TPs, the brash little wedge-shaped creatures who sprang from the Trivial Pursuit™ package hungry for one thing…Trivia! And as long as Horn and Abbot are on the case, the TPs will never go hungry.

So sit back, make yourself comfortable, and ask yourself the first question: How have I lived without this book for so long?

WHAT'S THE MOST FILMED OF SHAKESPEARE'S PLAYS?

I'M TELLIN' YA, MORTIE, THIS SHAKESPEARE KID IS HOT! DIDJA SEE MACBETH? WELL THIS IS THE KID THAT WROTE MACBETH! YA INTERERESTED? GOOD. CALL ME MONDAY, WE'LL TAKE A MEETING.

CIAO, BABY!

HEE HEE!

HAMLET

WHO HAD HIS MOUTH PRESERVED IN CEMENT OUTSIDE GRAUMAN'S CHINESE THEATER?

I TOLD YOU TO MOVE THAT ROPE!

CAUTION: WET CEMENT

JOE E. BROWN

Official Comic Edition
Featuring Horn and Abbot

WHAT 1963 FILM SHOWED A PARTY OF ENGLISH SCHOOLBOYS DEGENERATING INTO SAVAGERY ON AN UNCHARTED ISLAND?

FOOD FIGHT!
GOTCHA!
YAAH!
GET HIM!

LORD OF THE FLIES

Official Comic Edition
Featuring Horn and Abbot

WHAT MOVIE SAW BURT LANCASTER PREACH: "JESUS WOULD HAVE MADE THE BEST LITTLE ALL-AMERICAN QUARTERBACK IN THE HISTORY OF FOOTBALL?

TACKLE HIM?! YOU TACKLE HIM!

ELMER GANTRY

Official Comic Edition
Featuring Horn and Abbot

Official Comic Edition
Featuring Horn and Abbot

WHAT BRITISH ACTOR LEFT HIS LEGACY ON THE SIGNS OF A FAST-FOOD FISH-AND-CHIPS CHAIN?

CHARLIE'S CHIPS and FISH & STUFF and EELPIE

BURTON'S BAKED POTATOES and EELPIE

DAVID NIVEN'S FLOUNDER and EELPIE and CHIPS

SIR RALPH'S SUSHI RAW FISH and CHIPS and EELPIE

ARTHUR TREACHER

Official Comic Edition
Featuring Horn and Abbot

WHO APPEARED IN 1939'S *INTERMEZZO* WITH UNPLUCKED EYEBROWS?

O.K., BABY, FACE THE CAMERA!

I AM FACING THE CAMERA!

HMMPH! LOW BROW HUMOR!

INGRID BERGMAN

Official Comic Edition
Featuring Horn and Abbot

WHAT COMES AT THE END OF A JAMES BOND MOVIE?

THE CREDITORS?

WHAT WAS THE LEAST FINANCIALLY SUCCESSFUL OF THE JAMES BOND MOVIES?

MISS MONEYPENNY! CAN I BORROW A DOLLAR?

I SHOULD'VE TAKEN THAT JOB WITH U.N.C.L.E.

SORRY, PAL, NO PAYMENTS, NO CAR... O.K., TAKE 'ER AWAY!

GET LOST, DOUBLE-O DEADBEAT!

ON HER MAJESTY'S SECRET SERVICE

Official Comic Edition
Featuring Horn and Abbot

WHAT WAS THE FIRST TENNESSEE WILLIAMS PLAY FILMED?

WHIRRRR

SIR! WOULD YOU MIND REMOVING YOUR CAMERA?

SIR! WOULD YOU MIND REMOVING YOUR HEAD?

THE GLASS MENAGERIE

Official Comic Edition
Featuring Horn and Abbot

WHO WANTED HIS LINES INSCRIBED ON MARIA SCHNEIDER'S BACKSIDE FOR THE FILMING OF LAST TANGO IN PARIS?

I'LL DO IT! I'M THE HEAD CUE-CARD MAN!

I'LL DO IT! I'M THE DIRECTOR!

I'LL DO IT! I'M THE PRODUCER!

ME!

NO, ME!

MARLON BRANDO

Official Comic Edition
Featuring Horn and Abbot

WHAT HORSE HAS HIS HOOVES IMMORTALIZED IN CEMENT?

@∂@#?!!

HEH HEH!

MEN AT WORK

I'M IMMORTAL, TOO! I'M IMMORTAL, TOO!

Official Comic Edition
Featuring Horn and Abbot

WHAT BASEBALL MANAGER DID ACTRESS LORRAINE DAY MARRY?

CUT! WHO TOLD YOU TO SLIDE INTO THE BEDROOM?

SORRY, FORCE OF HABIT!

SAFE!

LEO DUROCHER

Official Comic Edition
Featuring Horn and Abbot

WHAT AIRLINE INTRODUCED REGULAR IN-FLIGHT MOVIES?

HEY, NO NECKING IN THE BALCONY!

IN FIRST CLASS THEY HAVE BUTTERED POPCORN!

WOULD YOU CARE FOR A NECCO WAFER?

WHAT DID MR. LUCKY ALWAYS CARRY WITH HIM?

LET'S SEE... I'VE GOT MY RABBIT'S FOOT, MY RABBIT'S *HEAD*, MY LUCKY RACCOON'S TORSO, MY LUCKY GORILLA EARS, MY LUCKY ELEPHANT TRUNK AND MY LUCKY HACKSAW...

LUCKY YOU!

WHO ARE YOU?

HIS LUCKY DUCKY.

A ROLL OF DIMES

Official Comic Edition
Featuring Horn and Abbot

O.K., GUYS, DRILL! WHAT COLOR DID MAE WEST WEAR IN PUBLIC?

WHITE!

WHO WAS OGLED AS *THE OOMPH GIRL?*

ANNE SHERIDAN.

WHAT DWARF RECEIVED AN OSCAR NOMINATION FOR BEST SUPPORTING ACTOR FOR HIS FILM DEBUT IN *SHIP OF FOOLS?*

DOPEY!

DOPEY?

I WAS *SURE* IT WAS GRUMPY!

WHAT PRESENTATION METHOD MADE ITS FIRST APPEARANCE AT THE 1940 ACADEMY AWARDS?

O.K. LET 'ER RIP!

SLAM!

IS THAT WHAT THEY CALL 'SHOOTING STARS?'

YEAH! 15 POINTS FOR A DIRECT HIT!

SEALED ENVELOPES

Trivial Pursuit™
Official Comic Edition
Featuring Horn and Abbot
HOW MANY PEOPLE FELL VICTIM TO THE SHARK IN JAWS?
WELL, ITS BEEN AN HOUR SINCE LUNCH. WANNA GO BACK IN?
DO YOU USE A WATERPIC?

WHAT DID JAMES CAGNEY IMPERSONATE IN HIS FIRST SHOWBIZ ACT?

YOU, YOU DIRTY RAT...

HEY, THIS IS REALLY EASY!

HE'S REALLY GOOD!

GOOD? HE'S UNCAGNEY!

FEMALES

WHAT WAS BING CROSBY'S GOLF SCORE THE DAY HE DIED?

YOU WANT TO GIVE HIM THAT LAST PUTT?

7

WELL... O.K.

EIGHTY-FIVE

Official Comic Edition
Featuring Horn and Abbot

WHERE DID COUNT DRACULA GO FROM TRANSYLVANIA TO BUY PROPERTY IN 1931's *DRACULA*?

WHAT A SUCKER!

O.K. LET'S SAY $500 FOR THE BRIDGE AND I'LL THROW IN BROOKLYN FOR AN EXTRA $250...

I'LL BITE!

BOOO! DON'T BOTHER TO RESCUE ME!

WANT TO JUMP IN THE TUB?

NO!!! WHAT IF WE LANDED IN THAT OTHER THING?

Official Comic Edition
Featuring Horn and Abbot

WHAT "FIRST" DID JOHN C. RICE AND MAY IRWIN PERFORM ON SCREEN IN 1896?

HOOO WEEE!

WOW! DOUBLE WOW!

ZZZ

WAKE ME UP IF THEY HAVE ANY DANCING CATS!

POPCORN

A KISS

HOW MANY FEET IN LENGTH MUST A MOVIE BE TO BE A FEATURE FILM?

WHAT DO YOU MEAN I'M SHORT?

I SAID "A SHORT," SIR. I SUGGEST YOU TRY THE TRAVELOGUE DEPARTMENT.

MEN'S WEAR

HELLO, RIALTO THEATER? DO YOU HAVE CITIZEN KANE IN A CAN?

3,000

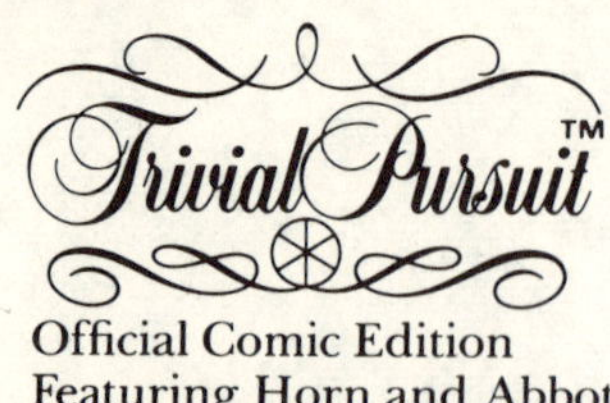

Official Comic Edition
Featuring Horn and Abbot

WHAT WAS THE FIRST WESTERN FILMED IN CINERAMA?

IF THIS KEEPS UP THEY'LL BE CHANGING THE NAME TO 16 MILLIMETER GULCH!

TAKE THAT, YOU WIDE-ANGLE WRANGLER!

POW!

HOW THE WEST WAS WON

Official Comic Edition
Featuring Horn and Abbot

WHAT KIND OF BIRD LAUNCHED THE FIRST ATTACK IN *THE BIRDS*?

WHY, YOU...!!

A SEAGULL

Official Comic Edition
Featuring Horn and Abbot

WHO NEEDS HANDLE BARS?

WHAT UNSIGHTLY FEATURE DID ABRAHAM LINCOLN HAVE ON HIS FACE?

THIS IS THE WORST PART OF BEING PRESIDENT!

GIDGET GOES TO ROME

I CAN'T WAIT FOR DADDY TO MEET TONY!

AFTER THIS WE'RE GOING TO SEE "I WAS A TEENAGE WEREWOLF!"

OH BOY! A DOUBLE FEATURE!

A WART

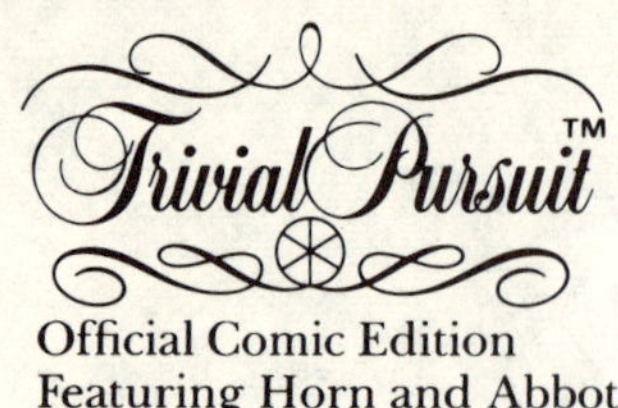

Official Comic Edition
Featuring Horn and Abbot

WHAT WAS MAE WEST'S BUST SIZE AT THE PEAK OF HER CAREER?

THE GREAT MAE WEST
+ ALL DOG BRASS BAND
+ HORN & ABBOT

THE GREAT MAE WEST
+ ALL DOG BRASS BAND
+ HORN & ABBOT

SURE SHE'S GREAT, BUT YOU SHOULD'VE SEEN HER TEN YEARS AGO!

EXIT

HOLLYWOOD OR BUST!

THIRTY-EIGHT INCHES

WHAT CHILD STAR WAS KEPT INTACT WITH FALSE FRONT TEETH AFTER HER BABY ONES FELL OUT?

O.K., VERY FUNNY! PROPS!

SHIRLEY TEMPLE

Official Comic Edition
Featuring Horn and Abbot

WHO KNEW ENOUGH ABOUT CARNAL KNOWLEDGE TO DIRECT IT?

FIVE MINUTES SIR!

MAKE IT TEN, O.K.?

Director

MIKE NICHOLS

Trivial Pursuit™
Official Comic Edition
Featuring Horn and Abbot
OH HORN! WHAT ACTOR HAS BEEN THE SUBJECT OF THE MOST BIO-GRAPHIES?
OH BOY! I LOVE QUESTIONS LIKE THIS!
LET ME THINK...
I'LL HELP!
FLUTTER
WELL?
SNAP
CAT GOT YOUR TONGUE?
AT LEAST I'M THOROUGH!
I KNOW IT'S CHARLIE CHAPLIN, I JUST CAN'T SAY IT'S CHARLIE CHAPLIN!

WHAT COUNTRY PRODUCED THE SO-CALLED "ANGRY YOUNG MAN" SCHOOL OF FILM?

WHAT'S MY MOTIVATION?

YOUR MOTIVATION IS THAT I SAID "ACTION" YOU STUPID HORSE!

BRITAIN

WHO DIRECTED *THE MALTESE FALCON*?

ALRIGHT, NOW REMEMBER YOU'RE A *STATUE*—THAT MEANS NO FLUTTERING, NO CROWING, NO *NOTHING!*

YOU MEAN THEY'VE CUT MY BIG LINE?

JOHN HUSTON

WHAT WAS SCOTT CAREY CHASED OUT OF BY A CAT IN THE INCREDIBLE SHRINKING MAN?

A DOLL HOUSE

O.K., GUYS, DRILL! HOW SHORT IS DUDLEY MOORE?

FIVE FEET, THREE INCHES!

WHO GREW UP IN CARVEL?

ANDY HARDY!

WHO PLAYED JOAN OF ARC FOR OTTO PREMINGER?

OOO, SOUNDS KINKY!

COME ON, NOW...

O.K., O.K., JEAN SEBERG!

STILL SOUNDS KINKY, THOUGH!

Official Comic Edition
Featuring Horn and Abbot

WHAT DO RECIPIENTS OF OSCARS PLEDGE NEVER TO DO WITH THEM?

"...NOR USE THEM TO UNCLOG DRAINS, CRACK WALNUTS, SQUASH BUGS..."

WELL I SHOULD HOPE NOT!

SELL THEM

Official Comic Edition
Featuring Horn and Abbot

WHAT DO YOU CALL A SHARK WITHOUT FRIENDS?...

ALONE SHARK!...

WHAT DIRECTOR ALWAYS HAD TEA ON THE SET AT 4 P.M.?

CUT! TEA BREAK!

ALFRED HITCHCOCK

WHO DID CLINT EASTWOOD PORTRAY IN HIS SPAGHETTI WESTERNS?

HEY, THANKS FOR THE FEED! WHAT DID YOU SAY YOUR NAME WAS?

I DIDN'T.

SLURP!

THE MAN WITH NO NAME

Official Comic Edition
Featuring Horn and Abbot

WHO PLAYED LOUIS ARMSTRONG IN THE FIVE PENNIES?

I'M FIRED?

IT'S GOT NOTHING TO DO WITH YOUR TRUMPET PLAYING, HONEST!

LOUIS ARMSTRONG

Official Comic Edition
Featuring Horn and Abbot

WHO RECIEVED THE ONLY OSCAR MADE OF WOOD?

SORRY, WE RAN A LITTLE SHORT ON GOLD THIS YEAR!

A WOODEN OSCAR?

WHY NOT? IT WAS A WOODEN PERFORMANCE!

I THOUGHT IT WAS JUST OAK-KAY!

EDGAR BERGEN AND CHARLIE McCARTHY

WHAT 1939 FILM REQUIRED THE SCREENTESTING OF 143 DOGS?

I'D LIKE TO DO MY SOLILOQUY FROM THE HAPPY-DOG DOG FOOD COMMERCIAL!

NEXT THREE! "FLUFFY" O'DWYER, "ROVER" NEWMAN AND "DUKE" SAPERSTEIN!

THE HOUND OF THE BASKERVILLES

Official Comic Edition
Featuring Horn and Abbot

WHAT 1967 ELIZABETH TAYLOR FILM TOOK PLACE AT A PEACETIME ARMY CAMP?

I CAN'T HEAR YOU!

YES, LIZ!!!

WHAT IF SHE ASKS ME TO SALUTE?

REFLECTIONS IN A GOLDEN EYE

Official Comic Edition
Featuring Horn and Abbot

WHAT MAGICIAN WAS BUSTER KEATON'S GODFATHER?

THIS IS THE LAST TIME YOU'LL SEE HIM SMILE!

HE'S A GREAT MAGICIAN! JUST DON'T ASK HIM TO MAKE YOU A SANDWICH!

TOO LATE!

HARRY HOUDINI

WHAT RAT WON THE AMERICAN HUMANE SOCIETY'S 1972 PATSY AWARD?

1972 PATSY AWARDS

CHEESE!

POP!

POP!

N38

Official Comic Edition
Featuring Horn and Abbot

O.K! WHAT IS AN OSCAR MADE OF?

WELL...?

BZZZ BZZZ BZZ

I'M WAITING!

UH... CHEESE!

CHEESE?!

SORRY, I PANICKED...

CHEESE?

CHEESE?

Official Comic Edition
Featuring Horn and Abbot

HOW MANY FINGERS WERE MISSING FROM HAROLD LLOYD'S RIGHT HAND?

THIS A NATURAL FOR A DOUBLE OR NOTHING BET...

OH, SHOOT!

AH-AH-AH... THIS IS MY *LEFT* HAND!

LET'S GIVE HIM A HAND!

ARE YOU KIDDING WE CAN'T EVEN GIVE HIM THE FINGER?

WHICH OF THE STARS OF *EASY RIDER* DIRECTED IT?

I SAID CUT!

DID HE SAY "CUT"?

I DIDN'T HEAR ANYTHING!

ROAR! VROOOOM!

DENNIS HOPPER

Official Comic Edition
Featuring Horn and Abbot

WHAT THREE PERFORMERS HAVE ALL WON OSCARS FOR PORTRAYING MUTES?

CLAP

THAT'S GOTTA BE A FIRST FOR THE ACADEMY AWARDS!

NO ACCEPTANCE SPEECH?

CLAP — — CLAP

JANE WYMAN, PATTY DUKE, JOHN MILLS

WHICH OF EDGAR BERGEN'S DUMMIES WORE A MONACLE?

THEN ONE DAY I WAS HAVING LUNCH WITH HOWDY DOODY, AND HOWDY SAID, "WHY DON'T YOU TRY CONTACT LENSES? I'VE BEEN WEARING THEM FOR YEARS."

I HEAR MISS PIGGY IS BLIND AS A BAT WITHOUT HERS!

WANT TO SEE ME TALK WITHOUT MOVING MY LIPS?

I'D RATHER SEE YOU MOVE YOUR LIPS WITHOUT TALKING!

CHARLIE McCARTHY

Official Comic Edition
Featuring Horn and Abbot

OH YEAH? WHICH WAS THE PREFERRED ONE?

WHO DUBBED THE VOICE OF FRANCIS THE TALKING MULE SIX TIMES?

BONJOUR

GOOD MORNING.

10 MILLION MULES AND THEY'VE GOTTA GET ONE THAT SPEAKS FRENCH!

CHILL MILLS

Official Comic Edition
Featuring Horn and Abbot

WHEW! I'M REALLY FLUSHED!

HAH! THAT REALLY BOWLS ME OVER!

WHAT FILM HAD KIRK DOUGLAS AND HIS HORSE RUN DOWN BY A TRUCK LOADED WITH TOILETS?

STOP THAT TRUCK!

ACME PLUMBING SUPPLIES

ZOOM!

LONELY ARE THE BRAVE

Official Comic Edition
Featuring Horn and Abbot

WHAT ACTOR INADVERTENTLY BLEW UP THE BRIDGE ON THE RIVER KWAI?

OH NO!

BOOM!

PLUNGE

ALEC GUINNESS

Official Comic Edition
Featuring Horn and Abbot

WHAT WAS PEYTON PLACE'S MAIN STREET?

GOODBYE, DOREEN!

'BYE, MR. ABBOT!

GOODBYE, HORN!

'BYE JEANETTE!

HI FOLKS!

I WONDER IF SHE SUSPECTS?

I WONDER IF HE SUSPECTS?

I WONDER IF SHE SUSPECTS?

I WONDER IF THEY SUSPECT?

ELM ST.

DR. ZHIVAGO'S FIRST NAME?

YURI.

WHO RECEIVED SECOND BILLING IN PSYCHO?

VERA MILES.

HOW MANY BUTTONS HELD UP MICKEY MOUSE'S PANTS?

PANTS?

LET ME EXPLAIN THE CONCEPT OF PANTS!

QUESTIONS AND ANSWERS FROM
THE ORIGINAL WORLD FAMOUS

BOARD GAME

CAN BE FOUND IN THESE OFFICIAL TRIVIAL PURSUIT™ COMIC EDITIONS:

BABY BOOMER COMIC EDITION
GENUS COMIC EDITION
ALL-STAR SPORTS COMIC EDITION
SILVER SCREEN COMIC EDITION

DON'T MISS THE WILD, WONDERFUL AND WACKY WORLD OF THE

COMIC EDITIONS
FEATURING HORN AND ABBOT.

AVAILABLE WHEREVER BANTAM BOOKS ARE SOLD.